Curious George
Goes Bowling

Adaptation by Cynthia Platt
Based on the TV series teleplay written by Raye Lankford

Houghton Mifflin Harcourt Publishing Company
Boston   New York

Friday night was bowling night. For George and the man with the yellow hat, this Friday was extra special. It was the night of the bowling championship.

Mr. and Mrs. Renkins and the Quints were bowling against the man, but who would win?

After the game, Mr. Renkins announced, "It's a tie! That means there will be a tiebreaker tomorrow night." George was so excited.

"Want to use my practice ball to roll one, George? I never let anyone use my lucky ball. It's the only one I ever hit a strike with!" said the man.

George rolled . . .

The next morning, George decided he wanted to help out—and polish the man's lucky yellow bowling ball for him!

George lifted the ball out of the bag and gave it a test roll. It rolled really well . . .

But then it kept on rolling—

Yuck! If that ball didn't need polishing before, it needed it now.

George worked hard. That kind of cleaning takes real monkey elbow grease.

Then the clean ball needed a test drive. George rolled it on the smooth, hilly driveway. But it was a little too smooth and hilly.

Later that evening, the man rushed to get his bowling bag and shoes. "George," said the man, "are you ready? We're running late."

They were just about to drive to Bowlmor Lanes when George realized that the man had taken the wrong bag. His lucky ball was in the other bag.

George jumped out of the car
and ran to get the ball . . .

George climbed a tree to think. The man needed his lucky bowling ball. But how could George get it to him? He had an idea. From the tree, the road to Bowlmor Lanes looked a little like a big bowling lane with gutters.

And if there was one thing George was good at,

With George's help, the man's lucky yellow bowling ball rolled uphill and down, and even had a close call with a passing flock of sheep.

Finally, it rolled right into the parking lot of Bowlmor Lanes and then through the front door

The ball rolled past the man with the yellow hat and down the lane—

and knocked over all the pins! "Oh, boy! He rolled that ball so fast, I didn't even see him wind up!" said Mr. Renkins.

Everyone celebrated, especially George. It was his best roll ever!